... g with travellers a wealth of experience and a passion for travel.

Rely on Thomas Cook as your travelling companion on your next trip and benefit from our unique heritage.

Thomas Cook **pocket** guides

INVERNESS

Thomas Cook

Your travelling companion since 1873

Written by Mike Gerrard and Donna Dailey

Published by Thomas Cook Publishing
A division of Thomas Cook Tour Operations Limited
Company registration no. 3772199 England
The Thomas Cook Business Park, Unit 9, Coningsby Road,
Peterborough PE3 8SB, United Kingdom
Email: books@thomascook.com, Tel: +44 (0) 1733 416477
www.thomascookpublishing.com

Produced by Cambridge Publishing Management Limited
Burr Elm Court, Main Street, Caldecote CB23 7NU
www.cambridgepm.co.uk

ISBN: 978-1-84848-468-9

This first edition © 2011 Thomas Cook Publishing
Text © Thomas Cook Publishing
Cartography supplied by Redmoor Design, Tavistock, Devon
Map data © OpenStreetMap contributors CC-BY-SA, www.openstreetmap.org,
www.creativecommons.org

Series Editor: Karen Beaulah
Production/DTP: Steven Collins

Printed and bound in Spain by GraphyCems

Cover photography © Thomas Cook Publishing

CONTENTS

SYMBOLS KEY

The following symbols are used throughout this book:

ⓐ address ❶ telephone ❶ fax ⓦ website address ⓔ email
❶ opening times ⓝ public transport connections ❶ important

The following symbols are used on the maps:

ⓘ information office		O	city
✈ airport		O	large town
➕ hospital		○	small town
🛡 police station		▦	motorway
🚌 bus station		—	main road
🚆 railway station		—	minor road
✝ cathedral		—	railway
▪ point of interest			

❶ numbers denote featured cafés, restaurants and venues

PRICE CATEGORIES

The ratings below indicate average price rates for a double room per night, including breakfast:
£ under £90 ££ £90–150 £££ over £150
The typical cost for a three-course meal without drinks, is as follows:
£ under £20 ££ £20–30 £££ over £30

❶ *Inverness lies in a beautiful setting on the River Ness*

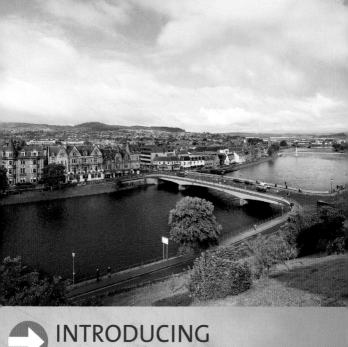

INTRODUCING
Inverness

Introduction

Inverness is the unofficial capital of the Highlands of Scotland, also known as the Gateway to the Highlands. It's a lively city on Scotland's northeast coast, at the mouth of the River Ness, which flows from Loch Ness through the city and out into the Moray Firth. Indeed, the name Inverness comes from the Gaelic *Inbhir Nis*, which means 'the mouth of the Ness'. The river certainly adds to the visual appeal of the city; here the Ness is wide enough to accommodate islands, which make for peaceful retreats from the city streets.

In those streets you'll find a bustling mix of locals and visitors. There are students from Inverness College, and Scottish visitors who come to the city for its shopping and entertainment. Other visitors have a wide range of accents and languages, as they travel from all over the world to holiday here, to enjoy the many outdoor activities right on Inverness's doorstep, to soak up the history of places like nearby Culloden and Cawdor Castles, and to see the wildlife in and around the Moray Firth. A few days in Inverness are invariably a part of their plans, and you'll often see people in hiking boots or carrying guitar cases.

This is nothing new. Inverness has always been a cosmopolitan crossroads, ever since it was settled about 5,000 years ago. Those settlers appreciated its position as the first fording point of the River Ness when it was at low tide. And while, over the centuries, it has absorbed aspects of many other cultures, its own Celtic traditions remain strong. The music sessions in its pubs may attract curious tourists in summer, but they go on all year round, and interest in Celtic culture has been developing rather than dying.

There may not be as many formal attractions as you might expect from a city of almost 60,000 people – it has only one museum, for example – but what it does have are a whole host of informal attractions, including some striking historic buildings, a riverside setting, traditional pubs, busy markets – and a constant stream of visitors.

The footbridge over the River Ness with the Free North Church beyond

When to go

SEASONS & CLIMATE

Inverness is a city best enjoyed in the spring, summer or autumn; those who like to pack a lot into their days will enjoy the long hours of daylight here in summer. The downside is, of course, winter, when it can feel dour and gloomy. Generally speaking, the climate is quite mild for the latitude.

Spring and autumn are good times to enjoy hiking in the hills and watersports such as sailing and kayaking. The midsummer months can be blighted by the curse of the Highlands – the midges. June to September are usually the worst months for these pesky creatures.

ANNUAL EVENTS

Burning the Clavie is when a half-barrel filled with tar and wood shavings is set alight and carried through the town of Burghead, an hour east of Inverness. It takes place on 11 January, the original date of Hogmanay in the Gregorian calendar (W www.hogmanay.net).

The Inverness Music Festival in March celebrates all aspects of Gaelic and Scottish culture with five competitive classes and a winners' concert in April (W www.invernessmusicfestival.org). Also in March, the **Inverness Half Marathon and Fun Run** begins in Inverness's Bught Park, with the route going by Inverness Castle and along the river before the runners head in the direction of Loch Ness (W www.invernesshalfmarathon.co.uk).

The **Inverness Summer Festival** is an umbrella term for many summer arts and cultural events in and around Inverness and

runs from June till September (Ⓦ www.invernessfestivals.com).
RockNess takes place in June, and is a 'monster' music festival
in every sense of the word, bringing tens of thousands of people
to Loch Ness (Ⓦ www.rockness.co.uk).

The **Inverness Highland Games** are usually held on the last
Saturday in July, featuring 'tossing the caber', throwing the Scots
hammer, and other unusual events in among the big athletics
programme (Ⓦ www.invernesshighlandgames.com). **Findhorn
Dinghy Regatta Weekend** is staged in July by the Royal Findhorn
Yacht Club in the lovely waters of the Moray Firth, off Findhorn,
51 km (32 miles) from Inverness (Ⓦ www.rfyc.net).

The **Blas Festival** is a big annual celebration of Highland life
and culture that takes place over ten days in September in and
around Inverness (Ⓦ www.blas-festival.com). The **Inverness
Winter Festival** stages cultural and other events, from
Hallowe'en to Hogmanay (Ⓦ www.invernessfestivals.com).

◯ *Enjoy the tartan finery at the Highland Games*

History

Inverness was first settled about 5,000 years ago by people who became farmers and fishermen, taking advantage of the fact that at low tide it was possible to ford the River Ness here. Some of the oldest known remains are the magnificent burial tombs at nearby Clava Cairns (see page 80), which date back to about 2000 BC.

🔺 *Inverness Castle: there's been a castle on this hilltop since the 12th century*

Inverness later became a stronghold of the Picts, and it was here that St Columba came in AD 565, converting the Pictish King Brude to Christianity. It is thought that the conversion might have taken place on the hill of Craig Phadrig, where a fort existed at the time.

In the 11th century, the centre of the city shifted to the hill by the river, where the original castle was built by the then King of Scotland, Malcolm III, at a point where a ferry crossed the river. By 1250 a bridge had been built and, outside the castle, Celtic monks founded a priory on St Michael's Mount, where the Old High Church now stands.

With its strategic location, Inverness grew as an important trading hub in medieval times, with a big shipbuilding industry too, and as a consequence it was much fought over. In 1652, Oliver Cromwell built a new citadel here, in his attempts to subdue the use of Gaelic and replace it with English. When the monarchy was restored, the citadel was demolished, to be replaced by the original Fort George in 1727. This was destroyed in February 1746 during the Jacobite Rising, and later a new larger Fort George was built at Ardersier, about 18 km (11 miles) northeast of the city.

In 1835 the present Inverness Castle was constructed during an economic boom, helped initially by the building of the Caledonian Canal and later by the arrival of the railways, which saw Inverness truly become the capital of the Highlands. The boom continues today; the population has doubled since 1980, and Inverness was granted city status in December 2000, thereby becoming Scotland's fifth city and the first new city in Scotland for 100 years.

Culture

As the largest city of the Highlands, Inverness has long been a centre for Highland culture. Traditional Gaelic music can be heard in the pubs and clubs around town most nights of the week; listen out too for the haunting sounds of *piobaireachd* – the classical music of the bagpipes. Music is not just there to be listened to, though: at pub ceilidhs, where music, singing and dancing all feature in the evening's entertainment, floors shake under the impact of energetic reels. In the music shops you can buy everything from CDs of Celtic music to your own set of bagpipes. And if you want to embrace the culture even more fully, you can head for one of the many local kiltmakers and get measured up for a bespoke Highland outfit.

It is not all about traditional culture, though. Travel to Inverness in June and you'll see people heading for the more contemporary music at the annual RockNess Festival, while Cawdor Castle stages music concerts by the likes of Westlife and the stars of *The X Factor*, while big names such as Rod Stewart perform at the Tulloch Caledonian Stadium.

The city's main visitor attraction, the Inverness Museum and Art Gallery, charts the history and culture of the city from earliest times to modern, as well as hosting regularly changing art exhibitions. There are also many fine contemporary art galleries showing works by modern Highland artists in painting, photography, ceramics and other media.

○ *The sun sets over the Moray Firth near Inverness*

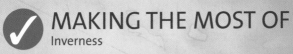

MAKING THE MOST OF
Inverness

Shopping

Inverness attracts people from all over the Highlands region who travel there for the shopping. For those who prefer out-of-town convenience shops, developments such as the Inverness Business and Retail Park – the location for big stores such as Tesco, Argos, Next and Comet – have sprung up on the edge of the city centre. Meanwhile, Inverness retains its traditional heart. Parts of the city are pedestrianised, and the whole centre is easily walkable, containing several specialist, independent stores of the kind that have closed down in many places.

Some of these retail outlets, such as a joke shop and a sewing shop, are in the delightful **Victorian Market**. This was built in 1890–91 and stands between Church Street, Academy Street, Queensgate and Union Street, close to the train station. In summer, a **farmers' market** sets up along the pedestrian High Street on the first Saturday of the month, and a **Continental market** operates here as well, though less regularly.

The modern equivalent of the Victorian Market is the **Eastgate Shopping Centre**, also close to the train station and containing many high-street chain stores such as Next, Monsoon, M&S, Debenhams, The Body Shop, HMV and Boots.

All around the town are Highland stores specialising in **kiltmaking**, as well as several good **outdoor clothing shops**. The city has the usual range of souvenir stores aimed squarely at visitors, so if you want to buy a Nessie doll or a miniature whisky with your clan name on it, you'll find it in Inverness. For more artistic offerings, check out the city's many fine little **art galleries**.

With its thriving music and Celtic culture scene, there are plenty of **music shops** where you can buy not only CDs but instruments too, like pipes and drums. Books on Scotland and the Highlands also make good purchases – if you can't find what you're looking for in a new bookshop, head for **Leakey's Bookshop** on Church Street, which claims to be the largest second-hand bookshop in Scotland.

⬤ *Take your pick of the tartan shops in the city*

Eating & drinking

Days in Scotland usually start with the chance to sample a 'full Scottish breakfast', after which you may not feel the need to eat again for hours, though vegetarians will be less happy with the focus on black pudding, haggis, bacon and sausages. Most hotels and guesthouses offer visitors this option, with some lighter choices too, like smoked salmon and scrambled eggs. Porridge is another essential part of the Scottish breakfast experience and can be served plain, with cream, with sugar, with salt, and even occasionally with a 'wee dram' of whisky mixed in.

Lunch can be taken any time from about noon to 15.00, with dinner often available from about 17.00 onwards, with some places closing by 21.00 (especially on dark winter nights), but

⬤ *A typical Inverness pub at lunchtime*

others staying open till late. Inverness hasn't always had the good range of dining options you'd expect from a fast-growing city, but in recent years that has started to change and now there is a wide choice from takeaways and fast food right through to the Michelin-star standards of the abstract restaurant (see page 53) and the Albert Roux restaurant, Chez Roux, at the Rocpool Reserve Hotel (see page 26).

In between the extremes of fast food and gourmet dining are many excellent eating places, especially around the **Church Street** and **Academy Street** areas in the city centre, along the river on Bank Street and on the opposite bank along **Huntly Street** and **Ness Walk**.

Scotland produces some fine food from its prime and pristine landscape; its salmon and venison, for example, are among the finest in the world. Scottish beef is particularly good, too. You'll find haggis – sheep offal mixed with onion, oatmeal and spices (much more appetising than it might sound) – on many menus, from breakfast through to dinner, with chicken and haggis a tasty combination. Vegetarians will have less choice, with just one token vegetarian dish being the norm, though an increasing number of places cater more seriously for vegetarians, and many chefs will be willing to accommodate requests.

Inverness has several parks where picnics can be enjoyed when the weather cooperates, and the town centre has both delis and bakeries that will provide the makings of a tasty meal and cafés serving takeaway treats. **Marello's fish stall** in the Victorian Market offers some ready-to-eat options, including smoked salmon in four different flavours (one of which is Drambuie), smoked mussels and seafood pâté.

Entertainment

Inverness doesn't have a huge number of large-scale venues, and entertainment is staged mainly at the smaller bars and clubs, where live music is a regular fixture. There's a healthy local music scene, particularly for traditional music, but also for indie rock bands.

There is no dedicated listings magazine for Inverness, but the Friday edition of the excellent and comprehensive local paper, *The Inverness Courier*, carries details of what's coming up. Also look for flyers in the many bars, clubs and music shops. The city is also small enough for you to get round and see what's on and what's forthcoming at most of the places that feature live music. Tickets for events should be obtained at the individual venues.

CINEMA
Eden Court (see page 61) tends to show the more arty films, with mainstream movies too, but blockbusters can be seen at the **Vue multiplex cinema** in the Inverness Retail Park.

LIVE MUSIC
There are many venues in the city centre offering live music, and you'll be able to find something on somewhere every night of the week. Indeed, some of the more famous venues like **Hootananny** (see page 55) have different music on different floors. Wander along **Church Street** and **Academy Street** and you'll find the music pubs and clubs; some of them look rather uninviting from the outside, but don't let that put you off. A certain amount of grunge is often part of their charm.

At the other end of the scale you also get major acts. Stars like Elton John and Rod Stewart have played concerts at the **Tulloch Caledonian Stadium** here, with an increasing number of pop concerts being held at nearby Cawdor Castle (see page 79), where Westlife were among the first big headliners.

THEATRE, OPERA & BALLET

Inverness has no regular ballet or opera, but Eden Court (see page 61) does welcome occasional visiting productions.

◆ *Eden Court: an important venue for cultural happenings in the Highlands*

Sport & relaxation

If there's one thing the city of Inverness does really well, it's sport. Among the many activities on offer are hiking, cycling, mountain-climbing and watersports. All are available right on Inverness's doorstep; there are also several golf courses nearby, angling opportunities right in the city itself, and many other options for watching or participating in sports.

PARTICIPATION SPORTS
Angling
You can fish in the River Ness right in the city centre, but you will need a permit, which you can buy at **J Graham and Co** (ⓐ 37–39 Castle Street). You can also buy all the fishing gear you need at this outdoor store, which was established in 1857.

Cycling
The route of the **National Cycle Network** passes right through Inverness and runs alongside the A9 as it crosses the Moray Firth. It heads into the Black Isle, while from Inverness another branch runs east to Nairn. There are numerous other cycle routes in the area and it's best to try to follow recommended routes: some of the roads here are not designed for sharing with cars. If you want to go mountain biking, then you can hire bikes and equipment at **A Ticket to Ride** in Culloden Moor (ⓦ www.tickettoridehighlands.co.uk). Bikes can also be hired from **Happy Tours** (ⓦ www.happy-tours.biz) whose rep can usually be found in front of the Inverness Visitor Information Centre. Look for the man in the kilt with a rickshaw.

⬛ *There is a large choice of cycle routes in the Inverness area*

Flying

You can take flying lessons or brush up on your flying skills by taking a plane out over Loch Ness, the Moray Firth and the Cairngorms at the **Highland Aviation Flying School** (ⓐ Unit 98, Inverness Airport ⓣ 01667 460361 ⓦ www.highlandaviation.com ⓔ info@highlandaviation.com ⓝ JET bus to airport).

Golf

There are three golf courses in Inverness and many more within easy reach.

Aigas Golf Course. A nine-hole course that sits amid gorgeous scenery. ⓐ Mains of Aigas, by Beauly ⓣ 01463 782942 ⓦ www.aigas-holidays.co.uk/course.htm ⓝ Bus: 28, 28A, 116, 307, 308 to Beauly

Cawdor Castle Golf Course. The castle's nine-hole course is set in mature parkland. ⓐ Cawdor, Nairn Ⓦ www.cawdorcastle.com Ⓛ 10.00–17.00 daily May–mid-Oct Ⓝ Bus: 1, X1, 252

Inverness Golf Club. This club has an 18-hole parkland course near the city centre and a clubhouse with two bars and a restaurant. ⓐ Culcabock Road, Inverness ⓣ 01463 239882 Ⓦ www.invernessgolfclub.co.uk Ⓝ Bus: 4

Loch Ness Golf Course. On the south side of Inverness, this offers an eighteen-hole course, a nine-hole family course and an all-weather driving range, bars and restaurant. ⓐ Fairways, Castle Heather, Inverness ⓣ 01463 713335 Ⓦ www.golflochness.com Ⓝ Bus: 5, 5A, 5B

Nairn Golf Club. A fabulous links course on the shores of the Moray Firth. ⓐ Seabank Road, Nairn ⓣ 01667 453208 Ⓦ www.nairngolfclub.co.uk Ⓝ Bus: 10A, 11 to Nairn

Hiking

An inexpensive booklet with walks around Inverness and Loch Ness is available at the Tourist Information Centre. Inverness is often a first stop for hikers moving on to the delights and challenges of walking in the Highlands. The **Great Glen Way** runs 117 km (73 miles) between Inverness and Fort William, along Loch Ness and the other lochs, and can be completed in 5–6 days. Within Inverness you can walk along the **river**, by the **Caledonian Canal**, or hike up **Craig Phadrig**.

Horse riding

Highland Riding Centre ⓐ Borlum Farm, Drumnadrochit Ⓦ www.borlum.com Ⓝ Bus 17

Highland Trekking and Trail Riding  Cougie, Tomich, Beauly
ⓦ www.cougie.com ⓝ Bus 28, 28A, 116, 307, 308 to Beauly

Spas

The newest spa in the city is at the Kingsmills Hotel
(ⓐ **Kingsmills Leisure Club**, Culcabock Road, Inverness
ⓣ 01463 257109 ⓦ www.kingsmillshotel.com). It has a fully
equipped gym, swimming pool, a sauna, steam room and spa
bath, and offers massages. There is also a **Spa and Leisure Club**
at the Best Western Palace Hotel (ⓐ 8 Ness Walk ⓣ 01463 223243
ⓦ www.invernesspalacehotel.co.uk).

Swimming & indoor leisure

Inverness Leisure has both a leisure pool and a competition pool.
The leisure pool includes a wave pool and a water channel
connecting it to the outdoor pool. There is also an area for
babies and younger children. Other facilities include a climbing
wall, gym, a running track and a sports hall that is big enough
for all kinds of activities, including football, gymnastics and
badminton. ⓐ Bught Park ⓣ 01463 667500
ⓦ www.invernessleisure.co.uk ⓝ Bus: 1, 12

SPECTATOR SPORTS
Football

Football is played at the Tulloch Caledonian Thistle Stadium, the
home of **Inverness Caledonian Thistle FC**, which competes in
the Scottish Premier League. ⓐ Tulloch Caledonian Stadium,
East Longman ⓣ 01463 222880 ⓦ www.ictfc.co.uk ⓛ (ticket
office) 10.00–16.30 Mon–Fri ⓝ Train: Inverness

Accommodation

There is plenty of accommodation in Inverness, particularly at the more budget end of the market; many streets in and around the town are lined with guesthouses offering bed and breakfast, so unless you are wishing to stay in peak season it should be possible to find somewhere without booking ahead. Otherwise the city offers everything from hostels and camping through to luxury and boutique business hotels – though there is less choice at the top end of the price range.

VisitScotland, who run the **Inverness Tourist Information Centre**, offer an accommodation booking service there (see page 93). The staff at the centre are incredibly knowledgeable about all the local options and will try to find you what you want. There is a small fee for this service.

CARAVANNING & CAMPING

Auchnahillin Caravan and Camping Park £ Set in 4 ha (10 acres) of a peaceful glen 13 km (8 miles) south of Inverness with pitches for tents, caravans and motor homes, and with caravans available for rent as well. ⊕ Daviot East ⊕ 01463 772286 ⊕ www.auchnahillin.co.uk ⊕ info@auchnahillin.co.uk ⊕ Apr–Oct

Culloden Moor Caravan Club Site £ A member of the Caravan Club and open all year, with a view over the Nairn Valley. There are 97 pitches with 80 of them hard-standing, and camping facilities, too, all about 10 km (6 miles) from Inverness. ⊕ Newlands, Culloden Moor ⊕ 01463 790625 ⊕ www.caravanclub.co.uk. ⊕ Open all year

HOSTELS

Eastgate Backpackers Hostel £ A 36-bed hostel with a fully equipped kitchen, lounge, dining room, TV and bike hires.
ⓐ 2nd floor, 38 Eastgate ⓣ 01463 718756
ⓦ www.eastgatebackpackers.com

Inverness Student Hostel £ This cosy hostel overlooking the river has 50 beds, lounge and kitchen. ⓐ 8 Culduthel Road
ⓣ 01463 236556 ⓦ www.invernessstudenthostel.com
ⓔ inverness@scotlandstophostels.com

HOTELS

Inverness

Lyndon Guest House £ The rooms in this smart and tasteful guesthouse have flat-screen TV, free Wi-Fi, en-suite bathroom and tea- and coffee-making facilities. ⓐ 50 Telford Street
ⓣ 01463 232551 ⓦ www.invernessbedandbreakfast.com
ⓔ lyndon@invernessbedandbreakfast.com ⓝ Bus: 28

Moyness House £ This Victorian villa was once the home of the writer Neil M Gunn. There is private parking and all rooms are en-suite with digital TVs, free Wi-Fi and CD players.
ⓐ 6 Bruce Gardens ⓣ 01463 233836 ⓦ www.moyness.co.uk
ⓔ info@moyness.co.uk ⓝ Bus: 1

The Willows £ Delightful and friendly family-run B&B, in an old house but with modern rooms. Facilities include free Wi-Fi, ample parking and TVs with DVDs. ⓐ 10 Millburn Road
ⓣ 01463 241143 ⓔ gbryden01@btinternet.com ⓝ Bus: 1, 2, 3, 8

The Chieftain Hotel ££ Recently refurbished, the Chieftain has its own restaurant, the Juniper, as well as a lounge bar and a sports bar. All bedrooms are en-suite. ⓐ 2 Millburn Road ⓣ 01463 232241 ⓦ www.chieftainhotel.co.uk ⓝ Bus: 1, 2, 3, 8

Heathmount Hotel ££ The Heathmount has recently been given the boutique treatment – rooms now have facilities like in-shower TVs and iPod docks. There's an excellent restaurant and two bars. ⓐ Kingsmills Road ⓣ 01463 235877 ⓦ www.heathmounthotel.com ⓔ info@heathmounthotel.com ⓝ Bus: 5

The Glen Mhor Hotel £££ The rooms and suites in this old building incorporate many of its original features, but with modern additions such as Wi-Fi and luxury toiletries. The hotel has its own bar and bistro, while some of the rooms overlook the river. ⓐ Ness Bank ⓣ 01463 234308 ⓦ www.glen-mhor.com ⓔ enquiries@glen-mhor.com ⓝ Bus: 3

Kingsmills Hotel and Leisure Club £££ This 4-star hotel is next to Inverness Golf Club. The original building dates from 1786 and retains its historic feel, but the newly built Kingsclub is a luxurious modern addition, with spa, sauna, steam room, gyms and swimming pool. ⓐ Culcabock Road ⓣ 01463 237166 ⓦ www.kingsmillshotel.com ⓔ info@kingsmillshotel.com ⓝ Bus: 4

Rocpool Reserve £££ Undoubtedly one of *the* places to stay in Inverness. With its Albert Roux restaurant and the r bar

cocktail bar, the Rocpool is a place of understated boutique elegance. All guest rooms have free Wi-Fi and all the luxury touches you might expect of an award-winning hotel.
ⓐ 14 Culduthel Road ⓣ 01463 240089 ⓦ www.rocpool.com
ⓔ info@rocpool.com ⓝ Bus: 5C, 7

Out of town

Strathview £ There are indeed breathtaking views over the strath from this wonderful little B&B that provides facilities way beyond its price range, including toiletries, free Wi-Fi and an iPod dock in the rooms. It's off the A9 but in a peaceful location, and owners Tom and Mary Semple couldn't be more helpful. ⓐ Cambusavie, Dornoch ⓣ 01408 633002 ⓦ www.strathviewbb.co.uk ⓝ Bus: X99 to Dornoch

Knockomie Hotel ££ Once the country home of the Earl of Moray, this is a romantic retreat in 1.5 ha (4 acres) of gardens. It's won several awards, including one for Customer Care, a sign of the attention guests receive. It's a good base for walkers who like their comforts, especially in the Grill Room Restaurant or Malt Library. ⓐ Grantown Road, Forres ⓣ 01309 673146 ⓦ www.knockomie.co.uk ⓝ Bus: 10A, 11 to Forres

The Lovat ££ What was an old-fashioned country-house hotel has been given an astonishing makeover. The Lovat has lost none of its traditional appeal, though, nor its comfort, with its spacious rooms, eco-friendly toiletries, and great location looking over Fort Augustus to Loch Ness. ⓐ Fort Augustus ⓣ 01456 459250 ⓦ www.thelovat.com ⓝ Bus to Fort Augustus

THE BEST OF INVERNESS

Although the city centre can be explored in a day or two, there are plenty of other attractions in the countryside around. Here are the sights you should not miss.

TOP 10 ATTRACTIONS

- **Inverness Museum and Art Gallery** The museum presents a fascinating overview of the city's history from ancient to modern times, while the gallery hosts shows by local artists (see pages 48–9).

- **The Victorian Market** A charming covered area with a range of interesting shops (see pages 47–8).

- **The River Ness** The river lies at the heart of the city and is one of Inverness's real delights. Walk across to the Ness Islands to enjoy a relaxing break from city life (see pages 44, 59 & 60–61).

- **Inverness pubs** Live music sessions are staged all year round; a night out in a music bar like Hootananny is a real Inverness experience (see pages 12 & 54–6).

- **The Caledonian Canal** A true engineering marvel that helped make the city what it is today (see pages 65 and 72–5).

- **Dolphin Cruises** Get a privileged view of these amazing creatures as they ply the Moray Firth (see pages 66–7).

- **Loch Ness** The loch has a 'monster' reputation; even without the lure of 'Nessie', this huge, beautiful loch would be a major attraction (see page 76).

- **Culloden Battlefield and Visitor Centre** Provides a fascinating look at the dramatic and complex story behind the 1746 battle (see page 80).

- **Clava Cairns** Burial tombs and a ring circle dating from about 2000 BC, located in beautiful and peaceful wooded settings (see page 80).

- **Cawdor Castle** Sits amid a vast estate; its stunning rooms and beautiful gardens make it one of the loveliest historic sites in the area (see page 79).

The Victorian Market is an atmospheric 19th-century shopping arcade

Suggested itineraries

HALF-DAY: INVERNESS IN A HURRY

Inverness is a small city, so it is easy to get a feel for the place
pretty quickly without having to rush around. Do visit the
Inverness Museum and Art Gallery, for a great overview of the
history of Inverness, and follow it with a walk along the river to
visit the **Ness Islands**. Wind up back in the centre to look in on
the **Victorian Market**; there are plenty of pubs, cafés and
restaurants around here for refreshment and relaxation.

1 DAY: TIME TO SEE A LITTLE MORE

With a day at your disposal, you can add a cruise on Loch Ness
to your half-day itinerary. **Jacobite Cruises** (see pages 67–8) will
pick you up at the bus station in the city centre, or on Bank Street
by the river, and take you out to their boat on Loch Ness for an
hour-long cruise on the loch. You can add in extra time to visit
Urquhart Castle (see page 77), if you wish, and still be back in
time for a meal and a music session in one of Inverness's pubs.

2–3 DAYS: SHORT CITY BREAK

To the 1-day itinerary, you can add in a **dolphin-watching cruise**
on the Moray Firth (see pages 66–7), where you should also
see seals and lots of seabirds. Again, complimentary transport
is available to take you from the city centre out to Inverness
Harbour and the cruise boats. Take in the Caledonian Canal
too, to see the **Muirtown Locks** (see page 65), and also the
three essential nearby highlights: **Culloden**, **Cawdor Castle**
and **Clava Cairns**.

LONGER: ENJOYING INVERNESS TO THE FULL

Longer visits to Inverness allow not only a chance to enjoy the city but also to take in some of the outstanding nearby scenery and attractions. At least two days should be given to exploring **Loch Ness**, if possible, perhaps spending a night in **Fort Augustus** (see pages 75–6) at the far end of the loch. A similar time can be spent exploring the **Black Isle** (see page 84), the peninsula north of the city that stands between the Moray Firth and the Cromarty Firth. Travel on a little further to the attractive seaside and golfing town of **Dornoch** (see page 87), with its small but impressive cathedral, before returning to Inverness.

⬛ *Loch Ness near Fort Augustus*

Something for nothing

Many of the attractions in and around Inverness are free of charge, so there is plenty to do if your budget is limited. Inverness Museum and Art Gallery is free to all visitors at the moment. Check before you visit, though, as, with impending budget cuts, this could change.

If the weather is clement, walk by the river and across to the relaxing Ness Islands, to prove that some of the best things in life are indeed free. The Caledonian Canal, at almost 100 km (62 miles) long, is one of Thomas Telford's great engineering triumphs; it heads southwest from Beauly Firth through Muirtown Basin, where you can admire the Muirtown Locks – and view other people's costly boats and barges.

To the west of the city, Craig Phadrig provides a bird's-eye view of Inverness and the Beauly Firth from its 100-m (328-ft) summit. An Iron Age fort stood here at one time, and if the lives and times of our ancestors interest you, then a visit to Clava Cairns is a must. The burial tombs, in a beautiful wooded setting, are a free time machine transporting your mind back 4,000 years to when they were built. Or head for the Merkinch Local Nature Reserve (see page 68), a 55-ha (135-acre) nature reserve that is a real city gem, with deer, owls, kingfishers, cormorants and many other creatures.

When it rains

It's possible to encounter rainy days at any time of year in Inverness, so it's best to be prepared with some options for what to do if and when that happens. There are plenty of indoor shopping opportunities, from the old Victorian Market to the large and modern Eastgate Shopping Centre (see page 50), just a few minutes apart. Leakey's on Church Street is said to be the biggest second-hand bookshop in Scotland, so bibliophiles will have no trouble spending hours here, fortified by good food from their café.

If you're feeling in a loftier frame of mind, then take a look around Old High Church (see page 47), the oldest in the city, from whose clock tower the nightly curfew bell still rings out. Or satisfy your curiosity and take a tour of some of Inverness's architectural gems: Inverness Castle (see page 46) and the ornate Victorian Gothic Inverness Town House (see page 47) are both working office buildings, but there are tours of them at regular intervals. Enquire at the Inverness Tourist Information Centre (see page 93) for details.

If you need to burn off some energy, or simply want to relax, head for Inverness Leisure (see page 58). Be as active or as inactive as you like – the centre boasts a swimming pool, gym and climbing wall as well as a relaxing sauna and steam room.

On arrival

ARRIVING
By air
Inverness Airport is about 13 km (8 miles) northeast of the city centre, so you can either hire a taxi or catch the JetBus, which takes you to Strothers Lane, alongside the main bus station and close to the train station. There is no train station at the airport. Buses run at roughly 15 minutes to and 15 minutes past the hour. There's also a bus service to Elgin, and several car rental companies. Other companies will also arrange to deliver and collect a hire car at Inverness Airport. Facilities in the terminal include a café, a restaurant/bar, an information desk and shops.

By bus
Coaches arrive daily from Edinburgh and Glasgow at Inverness Bus Station (ⓐ off Academy Street). Journey time is about four hours from both Glasgow and Edinburgh, depending on the company and particular service taken.

By car
The main road, the A9, passes right through Inverness from north to south, though it bypasses the city centre. The A82 goes off the A9 and takes drivers into the city from here. Other options include the A96 (if you are coming from Nairn and the east), which also meets up with the A9, and the A82, which runs parallel to the Caledonian Canal and Loch Ness to the southwest, goes through the city and out to meet the A9 on the other side.

Driving in the city is fairly straightforward, though it has its busy periods like any other place. There are several one-way streets but they are well-marked, although the area where Academy Street passes the Eastgate Centre and becomes Millburn Road can be confusing. The High Street is pedestrianised and the one-way systems take you around this.

There is very little on-street parking in the city centre, and most people use one of the multi-storey car parks. The Rose Street car park is next to the bus station and is one of the cheapest for long-stay parking. There is also a handy car park between the cathedral and Eden Court, on the west side of the river.

By rail

Taking the train to Inverness is a wonderful way to arrive. The Caledonian Sleeper service from London means you sleep through the night and wake up in Scotland, seeing some of the

🔺 *The railway station at Inverness*

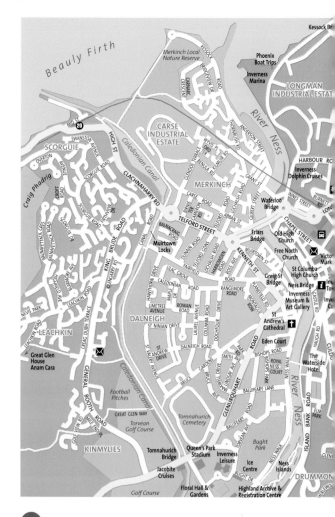

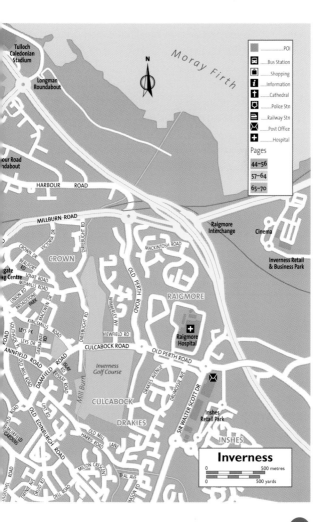

Moray Firth

	.......POI
	......Bus Station
	........Shopping
	........Information
	........Cathedral
	........Police Stn
	......Railway Stn
	........Post Office
	........Hospital

Pages
44–56
57–64
65–70

Tulloch Caledonian Stadium

Longman Roundabout

our Road ndabout

HARBOUR ROAD

MILLBURN ROAD

Raigmore Interchange

Cinema

CROWN DR

VICTORIA DR

DIRIEBUGHT RD

MACKINTOSH ROAD

CROWN

Inverness Retail & Business Park

gate g Centre

BEAUFORT RD

LOVAT ROAD

MIDMILLS ROAD

LINDON RD

BROADSTONE PARK

MACEWEN DR

DAMANWAY

OLD PERTH ROAD

WIMBERLEY WY

RAIGMORE

KINGSMILLS ROAD

LEYS PK

LEYS DR

DIRIEBUGHT RD

VIEWFIELD RD

Raigmore Hospital

ROAD

SOUTHSIDE

ANNFIELD ROAD

DALNEIGH RD

DAMFIELD ROAD

B&W

FERSKA ROAD

CULCABOCK ROAD

OLD PERTH ROAD

ANNFIELD ROAD

OLD MILL ROAD

Mill Burn

Inverness Golf Course

DRAKIES AVENUE

DRUMOSSIE AVE

SIR WALTER SCOTT DR

UST RD

CULCABOCK

Inshes Retail Park

FIELD ROAD

OLD EDINBURGH ROAD

MUIRFIELD GARDENS

DRAKIES

OLD MILL LANE

HARRIS ROAD

MILTON CRESCENT

TEAL AVE

INSHES

QUITHEL ROAD

DRINE AVE

DRUID RD

DELL ROAD

JOHNSTON RD

Inverness

| 0 | | 500 metres |
| 0 | | 500 yards |

37

Highlands scenery over an early breakfast, before arriving in Inverness at about 08.30. Single and twin-berth cabins are available, all non-smoking, and with a washbasin and shaver point. More comfortable first-class cabins are also available. If you are planning to travel with children, see the Sleeper Trains section of the ScotRail website (Ⓦ www.scotrail.co.uk).

Inverness Railway Station is in the centre of town, with taxis to take you to hotels and guesthouses if necessary. The bus station is only a one-minute walk from the train station.

FINDING YOUR FEET

If you arrive at either the bus or the train station, both are off one of the city's main streets, Academy Street. Cross Academy Street and keep walking and you'll pass through one of the busiest parts of the city, and end up by the river. Many of the city's main features are in or near this central area.

Inverness has its share of crime, like any main city, and while this central area isn't especially dangerous, the proximity of the bus and train stations to the busy central streets makes it a good place for pickpockets to hang out. Be vigilant, though, and you shouldn't be troubled by anything worse than someone asking for some spare change.

ORIENTATION

The main city centre is on the east side of the River Ness, in several blocks of streets between the river and Academy Street. Here you'll find much of the shopping and the bars and restaurants. East from Academy Street you'll also find the bus station, train station and library, all close together.

◓ *Inverness Bus Station stands next to the classical-style public library*

At the southern end of this city centre area is the Tourist Information Centre, Museum and Art Gallery, and Inverness Castle, also all very close together. East from the Tourist Information Centre runs the pedestrianised High Street, another main shopping street, with the Eastgate Shopping Centre more or less marking its eastern end.

There is still lots to find outside that central area, with the West Bank of the River Ness in particular having plenty of restaurants and nightlife, but if you can find your way round that central block and along either side of the river, you shouldn't get lost. If you do, look for Inverness Castle as a central landmark, or one of the four bridges that link the city centre to the west side of the river.

GETTING AROUND

Buses to the city centre run from Inverness Bus Station (off Academy Street) along Queensgate and Union Street. You can pick up a schedule of bus routes at the bus station. There are several different-numbered bus guides, and Guide 7 gives the bus services in the city and surrounding areas. There is no metro or light rail alternative, so the only transport options within the city are buses, taxis and walking. Fortunately, most of the main sites are within easy walking distance of each other.

Car hire

If you're restricting your visit to Inverness itself, then you don't need a car. For a slightly longer visit, however, a car will make access easier to some of the nearby sights – like Clava Cairns, for instance, which you can only otherwise reach by taking the bus to Culloden and walking, or going by taxi.

If, however, you're planning a visit of more than a few days, then renting a car is highly recommended. There are good bus services between Inverness and the main out-of-town places, but the scenery here is so beautiful that you will want to stop and enjoy it, or explore it. To get the most out of a trip, a car undoubtedly helps.

There are several local and national car hire firms in Inverness (see page 91). Expect to pay about £25–30 per day, or £160–190 per week, depending on the company, the car, and the time of year.

▶ Looking past the castle towards the city centre

THE CITY OF
Inverness

Introduction to city areas

The River Ness flows through the heart of Inverness, conveniently dividing the city centre. The East Bank is the pulsating heart of town, containing the city's main tourist attractions and many of its most popular restaurants and bars. It is also the retail hub of Inverness, with everything from quirky market shops to national high street chains and the sprawling indoor mall at the Eastgate Shopping Centre. The shops peter out on the West Bank, though there are plenty of good restaurants and bars on this side of the river. Many of the city's top cultural and leisure facilities can be found here, from the Eden Court Theatre to the Floral Gardens (see map on page 36).

Further west, the Caledonian Canal runs roughly parallel to the river. Although the surrounding neighbourhoods are solidly residential, here you can escape the city bustle and partake of the many outdoor pursuits that the locals enjoy, from cycling along the canal to hiking through the forests of Craig Phadrig, or visit the Clachnaharry Inn, one of the city's oldest landmarks.

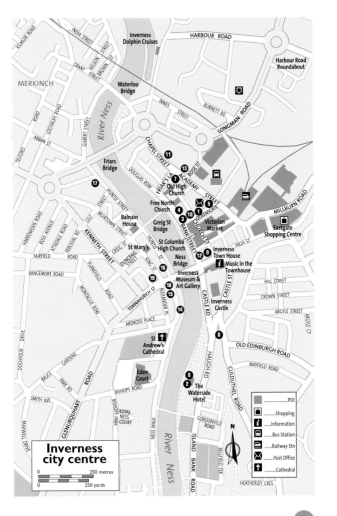

The East Bank

If you're a visitor to Inverness, the East Bank is likely to be your first stop and the place where you'll spend much of your time. This bustling part of the city centre contains the landmark Inverness Castle and the informative Inverness Museum and Art Gallery. The East Bank is quite compact and you can easily walk around it in an hour or less, though there will be much of interest to detain you along the way. Start at the castle, with its fine views over the River Ness, then wind your way from Bridge Street into the pedestrianised High Street and explore the surrounding side streets beyond.

SIGHTS & ATTRACTIONS

East Bank of the River Ness

With its ornate metal bridges and lush islands, the River Ness is the city's most scenic feature. Pavements along Bank Street and Castle Road run right beside the East Bank, providing pretty views and a perfect place to escape the city bustle. Walk south from Old High Church (see page 47), one of nine riverfront churches lining both sides of the waterway.

Opposite the Greig Street pedestrian bridge, the Gothic-style **Free North Church** (built 1889–92) boasts the tallest spire in Inverness. Further along is **St Columba High Church**, dating from 1852. Continue on to the Ness Islands (see page 59), where footbridges lead on to this shady retreat in the middle of the river. For a novel way to enjoy the views, **Happy Tours** offer rickshaw rides along the riverside (ⓐ Tours leave from the

⬥ A statue of Scottish heroine Flora MacDonald stands in front of Inverness Castle

Tourist Information steps ☏ 07828 154683 ⓦ www.happy-tours.biz ⓛ Daily by reservation ❶ Admission charge).

Inverness Castle

Since the 12th century, a castle has stood on this strategic hilltop. The medieval castle was captured and blown up by Bonnie Prince Charlie's forces during the 1745 Jacobite Rising. The present red sandstone castle was built 1833–6, with the northern section added a decade later. The **Inverness Sheriff Court** now occupies the castle and it is not open to the public, but there are fine views overlooking the river and the city from the surrounding grounds. ❸ Castle Hill

● *A view along Inverness High Street*

Inverness Town House

The turreted Town House is one of Inverness's most ornate buildings. Built in Victorian Gothic style, it was completed in 1882 for the Royal and Ancient Borough of Inverness. Today it houses the offices of the Highland Council, so its lovely artworks and historic features are generally inaccessible to the public. But guided tours are held twice a week in summer, enabling you to see the hidden treasures. ⓐ Corner of Bridge and Castle streets; for tour bookings go to the Tourist Information Office (see page 93) or Inverness Museum and Art Gallery ⓛ Tours 14.30 Tues & Thur (Jun–Sept) ⓝ All buses to city centre ⓘ Admission charge

Old High Church

Situated on St Michael's Mound, this is the historic town church of Inverness and the oldest in the city. A church has stood here since Celtic times, when St Columba is said to have preached here in the 6th century. While most of the present Old High Church was built in the 18th century, parts of the clock tower date back to the 14th century. From here, curfew still rings out at 20.00 every night. Spilling down the hillside is a large and atmospheric cemetery, where Jacobite prisoners were executed after the battle of Culloden.
ⓐ Church Street ⓦ http://oldhighststephens.com
ⓔ admin@oldhighststephens.com ⓛ Historic tours 11.30 Fri (Jun–Aug) ⓝ All buses to city centre

Victorian Market

Entering this covered market with its old-fashioned arcade of shops is a step back in time. After the original 1870 market was destroyed by fire, it was rebuilt in 1890 and is bordered by four city blocks, with entrances off each. The Academy Street entrance is the most striking, with Corinthian-style arches and carved animals on the keystones. There are more than 40 speciality shops, selling everything from bagpipes to jokes to Celtic music and gifts. Look for the toy train that runs around the top of the market, courtesy of the local model railway club. ⓐ Queensgate, Church, Union and Academy streets ⓦ www.invernessvictorianmarket.com ⓛ 09.00–17.00 Mon–Sat ⓝ All buses to city centre

CULTURE

Inverness Museum and Art Gallery

Housed in a modern building behind the Tourist Information Centre, Inverness Museum and Art Gallery is the city's main visitor attraction. Inside is a treasure trove of information on Inverness from its earliest beginnings, and an exploration of the history, natural history and culture of the Highlands. Among the displays on the ground floor are examples of the mysterious carved Pictish symbol stones, exhibits on Inverness during medieval times, and dioramas (miniature 3-D scenes) of Highland wildlife and habitats. Upstairs there are fine displays of Inverness silver, Jacobite miniatures, Highland costume and weaponry, and a re-creation of an early 20th-century Inverness kitchen. The art gallery, also on the first floor, stages a variety of changing exhibitions, mainly featuring local artists. ⓐ Castle Wynd ⓣ 01463 237114 ⓦ www.inverness.highland.museum

contact@invernessmuseum.com 🕐 10.00–17.00 Mon–Sat

All buses to city centre

Music in the Town House

Inverness Chamber Music holds a series of annual concerts in the Town House from September to April, featuring talented ensembles and solo artists from around Scotland and beyond. The Town House is also the venue for the monthly **Music at Lunchtime** series, whose performers range from guitarists and pianists to the Scottish Tango Ensemble. Corner of Bridge and Castle streets; for bookings contact James Munro,

🔺 *Leakey's Bookshop has a café as well as plenty of reading material*

Balnabruaich, 89 Culduthel Road, Inverness IV2 4HH ☎ 01463
710363 ✉ jamesmunro24@aol.com Ⓝ All buses to city centre
❗ Admission charge

RETAIL THERAPY

Chisholm's Highland Dress Top-quality goods are made on the
premises of this family run business, including kilts, jackets,
tartans and accessories. ⓐ 47–51 Castle Street ☎ 01463 234599
ⓔ info@kilts.co.uk Ⓝ All buses to city centre

Craigdon Mountain Sports Stocks a huge range of outdoor
equipment, from camping gear to winter sports clothing,
including children's clothing and equipment. The staff
give knowledgeable advice and also offer a boot-fitting
service. ⓐ 78 Academy Street ☎ 01463 248600
Ⓦ www.craigdonmountainsports.com
ⓔ sales@craigdonmountainsports.com Ⓝ All buses to
city centre

Eastgate Shopping Centre Anchored by Marks & Spencer and
Debenhams department store, Eastgate is Inverness's main
central shopping centre. There are a number of eating and
drinking venues here. ⓐ Eastgate ☎ 01463 226457
Ⓦ www.eastgate-centre.co.uk ⓔ info@eastgate-centre.co.uk
Ⓝ All buses to city centre

High Street Pedestrian Zone The traffic-free High Street is the
'main drag', running from the end of Bridge Street up to the

Eastgate Shopping Centre. Along here and in the surrounding streets you'll find around 500 shops, from small family businesses selling distinctly Scottish wares to national chain stores. High Street is lined with market stalls during the Farmers' Market, held the first Saturday of the month in summer, and the less regular Continental Market.

Leakey's Bookshop An Inverness institution, this quirky second-hand bookshop is located in the Old Gaelic Church, which dates from the 17th century. Stained glass, wooden floorboards and dusty shelves piled high with potential finds make this an atmospheric spot for book-lovers and browsers. The café on the mezzanine serves drinks, snacks and home-cooked lunches. @ Greyfriar's Hall, Church Street ☎ 01463 239947 🕐 10.00–17.30 Mon–Sat (café closes 16.30) 🚍 All buses to city centre

The Music Shop You'll be able to make your own music with The Music Shop's huge selection of sheet music and the instruments to play it on, from guitars to bagpipes. @ 27 Church Street ☎ 01463 233374 @ themusicshop@lineone.net 🚍 All buses to city centre

Riverside Gallery With a lovely location beside the River Ness, this gallery's extensive selection of oil paintings and watercolours ranges from 19th-century Scottish art to contemporary Scottish works, both modern and traditional. Browsers are welcome. @ 11 Bank Street ☎ 01463 224781 🌐 www.riverside-gallery.co.uk @ info@riverside-gallery.co.uk 🚍 All buses to city centre

TAKING A BREAK

The Room £ ❶ Enjoyable mix of bar and restaurant, where you can enjoy just a beer or a glass of wine, or a meal from the simple but tasty dishes on the menu, which include Parmesan baked cod, Cajun chicken penne, and a whole range of burgers, salads and ciabattas. There's also entertainment on Friday and Saturday evenings. 🅐 73 Queensgate ☎ 01463 233077 🅔 theroom@hotmail.co.uk 🕐 Food served 12.00–21.00 daily, drinks 10.30–23.00 Mon–Thur, 10.30–01.00 Fri, 10.30–00.30 Sat 🅝 All buses to city centre

Conservatory Restaurant ££ ❷ The light and airy restaurant at the Waterside is a popular local choice for a special occasion, and serves lunch and high tea, as well as dinner, when the candlelit tables and views of the River Ness come into their own. The food is mainly traditional Scottish, including dishes like steaks, salmon and venison terrine, and some mouthwatering desserts. 🅐 Waterside Hotel, 19 Ness Bank ☎ 01463 233065 🅦 www.thewatersideinverness.co.uk 🅔 info@thewatersideinverness.co.uk 🕐 12.00–21.30 daily 🅝 All buses to city centre

The Mustard Seed ££ ❸ One of the most popular restaurants in Inverness, partly for the atmosphere created by its location in an old church building and partly for its superb food, which includes very flavoursome dishes such as baked fillet of halibut on smoked bacon with a saffron risotto. 🅐 16 Fraser Street ☎ 01463 220220 🅦 www.mustardseedrestaurant.co.uk

e info@mustardseedrestaurant.co.uk **L** 12.00–15.00, 17.30–22.00 daily **N** All buses to city centre

River Café & Restaurant ££ 4 Attractive and lively riverside eating place that serves cakes, pastries and snacks all day, with longer lunch, early evening and dinner menus, and high tea too. Contemporary twists on traditional Scottish dishes are a speciality, such as seared venison steak on a haggis mash. **a** 10 Bank Street **t** 01463 714884 **w** www.invernessrestaurant.com **e** rivercafeandrestaurant@yahoo.co.uk **L** 12.00–14.30, 17.00–21.30 Mon–Sat **N** All buses to city centre

The Steak Academy ££ 5 This stylish new place in the city centre prides itself on serving 'Scottish fare with a hint of the exotic'. As well as Aberdeen Angus steaks you can try ostrich, kangaroo or springbok, though non-carnivores can also choose from fish and vegetarian menus too. **a** 8 Queensgate **t** 01463 709409 **w** www.thesteakacademy.com **e** info@thesteakacademy.com **L** 12.00–14.30, 17.00–22.00 Mon–Sat (daily in summer) **N** All buses to city centre

abstract £££ 6 Undoubtedly one of the best restaurants in town, with an eight-course tasting menu, a Chef's Table where you can dine in the kitchen, and a regular à la carte menu offering locally sourced seasonal dishes. **a** 20 Ness Bank **t** 01463 223777 **w** www.abstractrestaurant.com **e** reception@glenmoristontownhouse.com **L** 18.00–22.00 Tues–Sat **N** All buses to city centre

AFTER DARK

Blackfriars Highland Pub ❼ Built in 1793 and once
a temperance hotel, today the Blackfriars is anything but.
Live traditional music most nights, including ceilidhs with the
Singing Landlord, and a great range of local real ales too.

ⓐ 93–95 Academy Street ☎ 01463 233881

ⓦ www.blackfriarshighlandpub.co.uk

ⓔ info@blackfriarshighlandpub.co.uk 🕒 12.00–23.00 daily

Ⓝ All buses to city centre

🔺 *Hootananny is the place to go for a musical evening*

Castle Tavern ❽ One of the most popular pubs in the city, for its good range of well-kept beers, the food in the quieter upstairs restaurant, and occasional live music, though mostly people see it as a meeting place where you can enjoy a good pint of beer. ⓐ 1 View Place ❶ 01463 718178 Ⓦ www.castletavern.net ⓔ enquiries@castletavern.net ❶ 12.00–22.00 daily for food Ⓝ All buses to city centre

Gellions Bar ❾ Easy to find opposite the Tourist Information Centre, Gellions has two bars where you can choose from live music at weekends, including a popular Saturday ceilidh at 17.00, or watch live sports on the big-screen TVs, have a meal (noon–midnight), or just a quiet drink. ⓐ 14–17 Bridge Street ❶ 01463 233648 Ⓦ www.gellions.co.uk ⓔ bars@gellions.co.uk ❶ 09.00–01.00 Mon–Sat & 12.30–24.00 Sun Ⓝ All buses to city centre

Hootananny ❿ Consistently voted the best pub in town by Invernessians, Hootananny is the place to go if you only have time to visit one music venue. There's different music in three music rooms, with traditional music most nights, and rock bands with a DJ upstairs. It has two bars and good Thai food as well. ⓐ 67 Church Street ❶ 01463 233651 Ⓦ www.hootananny.co.uk ⓔ info@hootananny.co.uk ❶ 12.00–late daily Ⓝ All buses to city centre

The Ironworks ⓫ This purpose-built city-centre venue has hosted music acts like The Proclaimers, and the 'bagpipers with attitude', the Red Hot Chilli Pipers, stand-ups such as

Jenny Eclair and Reginald D Hunter, and other events like wrestling. It's always worth checking their programme online ahead of a visit. ⓐ 122b Academy Street ⓣ 0871 7894173 ⓦ www.ironworksvenue.com ⓔ office@ironworksvenue.com ⓛ (box office) 10.00–18.00 Mon–Sat ⓝ All buses to city centre

Johnny Foxes ⓬ This bar and restaurant overlooking the river has food and occasional live bands, and is hugely popular with young locals. Food covers Thai, Scottish, French, Italian and more, and on a sunny day the terrace is the perfect hanging-out place. ⓐ 26 Bank Street ⓣ 01463 236577 ⓦ www.johnnyfoxes.co.uk ⓛ 12.30–24.00 daily ⓝ All buses to city centre

The Phoenix ⓭ One of the oldest and most traditional bars in Inverness, with Flames Restaurant and Music Venue adjoining, the Phoenix still has its original beer pump working but also has Friday rock nights, kids' menus – something for everyone. ⓐ 106–110 Academy Street ⓣ 01463 245990 ⓛ 11.00–01.00 Mon–Fri, 11.00–00.30 Sat, 12.00–24.00 Sun ⓝ All buses to city centre

The West Bank

Apart from the retail stretch along the riverfront, the West Bank quickly gives way to residential streets, many of which are dotted with B&B accommodation. But you'll still find several good restaurants and bars here too. St Andrew's Cathedral is among the riverside churches. Other attractions highlight the city's recreational and outdoor delights, from the Floral Hall and Gardens to the idyllic Ness Islands.

On the West Bank, there's no need to stray far from the river. A half-hour stroll south along the waterfront from Friars Bridge will bring you to all the main sights.

SIGHTS & ATTRACTIONS

Bught Park

Opposite Ness Islands, Bught Park is the largest city park in Inverness. Its big, grassy expanse makes it the perfect home for the annual Inverness Highland Games, and music concerts are also held here in summer. Within the park is the Bught Park sports stadium, home to the Inverness Shinty Club since 1934. Shinty is a field sport played with a small ball and sticks, and has similarities to field hockey and the Irish sport of hurling. Adjacent to the park is the Inverness Ice Centre, which offers ice-skating, ice hockey and curling in season. ❸ Fort Wilderness Road

Floral Hall and Gardens

Admire a range of plants and floral displays at Inverness's botanical gardens. The Floral Hall is a glasshouse containing subtropical plants and orchids, set around a tumbling waterfall and a Koi carp pool. There is a fascinating collection of live exotic insects and reptiles here too. The outdoor gardens feature a range of mixed plantings, arranged in creative, colourful displays. There is also a sensory garden, a rockery and garden project for people with learning disabilities, and a teddy bears' den for young garden lovers. ⓐ Bught Lane ⓣ 01463 713553 ⓦ www.invernessfloralhall.com ⓔ moreinfo@invernessfloralhall.com ⓛ 10.00–17.00 daily (Easter–Oct), 10.00–16.00 daily (Nov–Easter) ⓝ Bus: 12 from city centre ⓘ Admission charge

Inverness Leisure

Adjacent to Bught Park, Inverness's premier sports and leisure centre offers a variety of recreational facilities for all ages. There's a wave pool with water geysers, three flumes, a moving river, an outdoor pool with bubble jets, toddler pool and a family spa bath. There is an eight-lane, 25-metre competition pool for serious swimmers, and a Health Suite with sauna, steam room, spa bath and large relaxation area for serious chilling-out. On the dry side, the centre contains a gym, climbing wall, sports hall and studio class. The 400-metre all-weather running track in the adjacent Queens Park Stadium is also open to the public when not in use for events or group activities. Individual facilities are open to everyone on a pay-as-you-play basis, or on a monthly or annual basis. ⓐ Bught Lane ⓣ 01463 667500 ⓦ www.invernessleisure.co.uk ⓔ info@invernessleisure.co.uk ⓛ Hours vary by facility, see website ⓝ Bus: 12 from city centre ⓘ Admission charge

Ness Islands

In the early 1800s, the city fathers had the foresight to purchase the Ness Islands, preserving this natural beauty spot as a recreational retreat for the people of Inverness. Covered with mature trees, it serves as an important wildlife corridor between the Moray Firth and Loch Ness. Bats, otters and a variety of birds can be seen here, while the salmon pools make this a popular urban fishing spot in season.

You can cross to the islands from both the East and West banks. In recent years, local artists have enhanced the islands with sculpted benches, gateways and bridge balustrades that complement the natural woodland surroundings. Look out for the **General's Well**, one of several ancient healing wells once used in Inverness. The remnants of an open-air theatre can be found in the centre of the islands, where a variety of summer entertainment took place in the 1950s. The bridges and pathways are lit up again these days for the Ness Islands Lights show during the Winter Festival in December.

● *Enjoy walking or cycling on Ness Islands*

St Andrew's Cathedral

Set in a leafy square along the waterfront, the cathedral provides one of the city's prettiest riverside views. Its massive square towers, 30 m (100 ft) high, were meant to be topped by equally high spires, but were never finished. Built in 1866–9 to a Gothic Revival design by Alexander Ross, a church member, the airy interior has many features of interest. Each of the pillars that support the arches of the nave are carved from a single block of granite, with ornate carved capitals and carved faces above. The stained glass of the great west window, one of the largest in Scotland, retains its magnificent colours as it is protected from direct sunlight. In summer, the Old Boys' School behind the cathedral houses a tea room. **ⓐ** Ardross Street **ⓣ** 01463 233535 **ⓦ** www.invernesscathedral.com **ⓛ** 09.00–18.00 daily

West Bank of the River Ness

A stroll down the West Bank of the River Ness affords lovely views, particularly of Inverness Castle towering above. Begin on Huntly Street just below Friars Bridge. Between here and Ness Bridge, keep an eye out for seals, which sometimes swim in from the Moray Firth. Pass the historic **Balnain House**, an early Georgian town house that now houses the National Trust for Scotland office. Further along, past the Greig Street suspension bridge, is **St Mary's**, the first Roman Catholic church built in the city after the Reformation. Built in perpendicular Gothic Revival style, it opened in 1837. Carry on to **St Andrew's Cathedral** and the **Eden Court** theatre. Keep to the riverfront along Ness Walk and, as you near the suspension bridge, you may see fishermen standing in the river, trying their luck in the salmon pools. Opposite Bught Park, cross the footbridge on to the Ness Islands. You can cross another bridge to return along the East Bank to the city centre, a circular walk of 1–2 hours, depending on how long you linger.

CULTURE

Eden Court

Eden Court is the largest performing arts venue in the Highlands, featuring drama, ballet, dance, opera, films and musical concerts. It was built on the grounds of the former Bishop's Palace, a Victorian house that has been incorporated into the complex. Recent renovations have made Eden Court thoroughly modern, from the striking riverfront landscaping leading up to the glass-fronted entrance to the new extensions, which provide a second theatre, two new cinemas, dance and drama studios and more. ⓐ Bishops Road ⓣ 01463 234234 ⓦ www.eden-court.co.uk ⓝ Bus: 12 ❶ Admission charge

Highland Archive and Registration Centre

Operated by the Highland Council Archive Service, this building holds a vast number of historical documents dating back to 1455. Most records can be accessed free of charge in the public searchroom. The Family History Centre focuses on genealogy, clan history and family history, throughout the region and around the world. Parish registers, census returns and other records can also be searched for free, including a collection of gravestone inscriptions from Highland burial grounds. ⓐ Bught

Road ☎ 01463 256444 ⓦ www.highland.gov.uk/archives
✉ archives@highland.gov.uk 🕐 Searchroom: 10.00–17.00 Mon,
Tues & Thur, 10.00–19.30 Wed; Family History Centre: 10.00–
17.00 Mon, Tues, Thur & Fri, 10.00–19.30 Wed Ⓝ Bus: 12
ⓘ Charges for photocopying and genealogical consultations

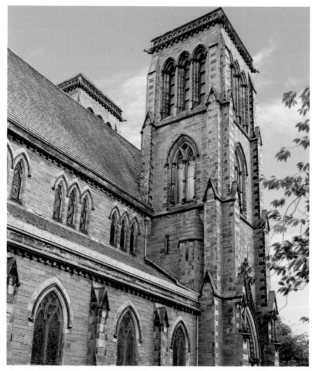

🔺 *St Andrew's Cathedral is an Episcopal cathedral on the river bank*

RETAIL THERAPY

Scottish Kiltmaker Visitor Centre A chance to buy kilts or other Highland wear, heraldic products and general souvenirs plus a display on the history of the kilt. ❸ 4–9 Huntly Street ❶ 01463 222781 Ⓦ www.highlandhouseoffraser.com ❷ info@highlandhouseoffraser.com ❸ 09.00–22.00 daily Ⓝ Bus: 12

TAKING A BREAK

McNab's £ ⓮ Part of the Columba Hotel next door but works successfully as a separate bar and bistro, attracting a wide range of locals. Really comfy easy chairs to lounge in, and a pub-style menu that includes fish and chips, venison sausage and mash, and the like. Also has music at the weekends. ❸ 7 Ness Walk ❶ 01463 231391 ❶ 01463 715526 Ⓦ www.oxfordhotelsandinns.com ❸ 12.00–late daily Ⓝ Bus: 12

Riva Restaurant and Pizzeria £–££ ⓯ The smarter restaurant is downstairs and the less expensive pizzeria upstairs, but they both serve exceptionally good Italian food, including delicious desserts like tiramisu flavoured with Tia Maria. ❸ 4–6 Ness Walk ❶ 01463 231391 Ⓦ www.rivarestaurant.co.uk ❷ rivainverness@btconnect.com ❸ 12.00–14.30, 17.00–21.30 Mon–Sat, 17.00–21.30 Sun Ⓝ Bus: 12

The Kitchen ££ ⓰ This modern restaurant offers great views of Inverness Castle through large plate-glass windows, or from the roof terrace. Enjoy outstanding meals such as breast of chicken on Highland haggis with a turnip and potato mash and a whisky and onion cream. 🄰 15 Huntly Street 🄣 01463 259119 🅦 www.kitchenrestaurant.co.uk 🄴 info@kitchenrestaurant.co.uk 🄾 12.00–15.00, 17.30–22.00 daily 🄽 Bus: 12

Waterfront Bar and Restaurant ££ ⓱ Informal bar and restaurant with a cosy atmosphere and a very nice menu. Dinner choices range from roast pheasant in season to chicken with haggis, steaks and seafood. Also lunches and bar meals. 🄰 70–71 Huntly Street 🄣 01463 233870 🄾 12.00–15.00, 17.00–21.00 daily 🄽 Bus: 12

Rocpool Rendezvous £££ ⓲ The original Rocpool Restaurant by the River Ness, serving contemporary Scottish cuisine. Possibly the best cooking in town, exemplified in dishes like loin of venison roasted with Parma ham and black pudding or rich chocolate and praline tart with toffee ice cream. 🄰 1 Ness Walk 🄣 01463 717274 🅦 www.rocpoolrestaurant.com 🄴 info@rocpoolrestaurant.com 🄾 12.00–14.30, 17.45–22.00 Mon–Sat 🄽 Bus: 12

AFTER DARK

Ceol Mor ⓳ Its name means 'big music' in Gaelic; this bar has a friendly Scottish atmosphere and serves food, too. Live music at the weekends and rock karaoke on Thursdays. 🄰 18 Tomnahurich Street 🄣 01463 250690 🅦 www.ceol-mor.com 🄾 11.00–13.00 Mon–Thur, 11.00–24.30 Fri & Sat, 12.00–24.00 Sun; live music from 21.00

The Caledonian Canal

Nature and wildlife are right on the doorstep in Inverness. So you will find some wonderful options for outdoor recreation, from dolphin watching on the Moray Firth to forested walks up Craig Phadrig or along the Caledonian Canal. These outlying places of interest are best reached by car, but some are on or near bus routes from the city centre.

SIGHTS & ATTRACTIONS

The Caledonian Canal

The Caledonian Canal has its northern terminus in Inverness and is a great recreational asset to the city. The canal joins the Beauly Firth at Clachnaharry. It flows south through a wide section called the Muirtown Basin, where you can see a variety of boats in the marina. Below the swing bridge over Telford Street are the Muirtown Locks, a flight of four.

In the city, the prettiest section of the canal lies south of the Tomnahurich Bridge (Glenurquhart Road), where it swings round to run parallel to the River Ness. A favourite walk is along the towpath on the south bank of the canal, where it overlooks the river running at a lower elevation. You can follow it all the way to the locks at Dochgarroch, a distance of about 5 km (3 miles), and return up the other side.

Craig Phadrig

The steep, forested hill of Craig Phadrig rises to the west of the city. There are pleasant woodland paths winding up to the

● A dolphin leaps in the Moray Firth

top, a climb of about 100 m (328 ft), which will take about an hour. From here there are good views over Inverness and the Beauly Firth. The remains of a Pictish fort occupy the summit, which was built on the ruins of an even earlier Iron Age fort. Craig Phadrig is a vitrified fort, which means that its rock walls are partially fused together. It is thought that such strongholds were ritually burnt after they were captured, the timber framework reaching furnace-like temperatures that were hot enough to melt the rock. ❸ Craig Phadrig ◍ Bus: 28 to Clachnaharry

Dolphin watching

The Moray Firth is one of the best places to see bottlenose dolphins. **Phoenix Boat Trips** depart from Inverness Marina and take you out on the *Seacruise* to look for the dolphins and view the seals at Ardersier. From Shore Street Quay, **Inverness Dolphin**

Cruises ply the waters of the firth to watch for dolphins as well as ospreys, red kites and seals. If you prefer a shore-based wildlife tour, **Dolphin Watch** takes small groups (a maximum of six) to the best viewing spots along the Moray Firth to spot dophins, minke whales, basking sharks and more.

Dolphin Watch ☎ 0794 461 7562 ⓦ www.dolphin-watch.co.uk
ⓔ info@dolphin-watch.co.uk ⓝ Pick-ups from the Tourist Information Centre

Inverness Dolphin Cruises ⓐ Shore Street Quay
☎ 01463 717900 ⓦ www.inverness-dolphin-cruises.co.uk
ⓔ info@inverness-dolphin-cruises.co.uk ⓛ Mar–Oct, weather permitting ⓝ Courtesy bus from city centre

Phoenix Boat Trips ⓐ Inverness Marina, Longman Drive
☎ 01667 456078 ⓦ www.inverness-dolphin-trips.co.uk
ⓔ eric@drumblair.f9.co.uk ⓛ Easter–Sept, weather permitting
ⓝ Bus: 9

Great Glen House

Completed in 2006, Great Glen House is the headquarters for Scottish Natural Heritage. The building is highly acclaimed both for its innovative architecture and its sound environmental principles; with its timber-framed glass atrium and circular library, the low-carbon building is as striking as it is sustainable, and is frequently photographed. ⓐ Leachkin Road ☎ 01463 725000 ⓦ www.snh.gov.uk ⓔ enquiries@snh.gov.uk ⓝ Bus: 1, 2

Jacobite Cruises

The best way to experience the Caledonian Canal is from the water. Jacobite Cruises offers trips down the canal from

Inverness, with a cruise on Loch Ness as far as Urquhart Castle. Longer tours include a visit to the castle and other attractions. ⓐ Tomnahurich Bridge, Glenurquhart Road ⓣ 01463 233999 ⓦ www.jacobite.co.uk ⓔ info@jacobite.co.uk ⓛ Year-round, weather permitting Ⓝ Coach transfer from city centre

Merkinch Local Nature Reserve

Tucked away at the tip of South Kessock between the Caledonian Canal and the mouth of the River Ness, this delightful local nature reserve covers some 55 ha (135 acres) along the Moray Firth. Its reed beds, salt marsh, pools, woods, banks and bog provide habitat for a variety of wildlife species, from herons, kingfishers, cormorants and wading birds to owls, weasels and roe deer. Two main trails wind through the reserve, with a boardwalk, benches and interpretive panels along the way. Conservation volunteers help maintain the reserve during weekly Green Gym sessions. ⓐ Merkinch Partnership,

◔ *A lock on the Caledonian Canal near Inverness*

4 Grant Street ☎ 01463 718989 🌐 www.merkinchlnr.org.uk
✉ anne@merkinch.com Ⓝ Bus: 3, 3A

Tomnahurich Cemetery

This sprawling hillside cemetery, whose name means 'hill of the yews', dates from the 1850s. Alexander Ross, the architect of St Andrew's Cathedral, is among the notables buried here. The steep slopes make for quite a climb to the top, where a war memorial marks the highest point. According to local folklore, Tomnahurich Hill is home to the fairies. Among the many legends associated with it are tales of fiddlers who were taken inside the hill to play for fairy gatherings, only to emerge 100 years later. ⓐ Entrance on Glenurquhart Road

CULTURE

Anam Cara

Three miles from the city centre, this idyllic retreat centre has beautiful views over the surrounding countryside towards the mountains. Along with holistic therapies and counselling, the centre offers a range of classes, workshops, retreats and events in such disciplines as Buddhism, yoga and the healing arts. Visit the website to see the full programme. ⓐ 18 Upper Leachkin
☎ 01463 711702 🌐 www.anamcara.org ✉ welcome@anamcara.org

TAKING A BREAK

Clachnaharry Inn ££ ⑳ This traditional 17th-century coaching inn is at the west end of the city, just before you head out of town towards Beauly on the A862. It has log fires in winter and a sun terrace with beautiful views across the Beauly Firth. The pub is a local favourite for its real ales on tap and traditional music sessions – and serves great food, too. ⓐ 17–19 High Street ⓣ 01463 239806 ⓦ www.clachnaharryinn.co.uk ⓔ enquiries@ clachnaharryinn.co.uk ⓑ 12.00–14.30, 17.00–21.00 Mon–Sat, 12.00–17.00 Sun ⓝ Bus: 28

THE PICTS

The Picts, who effectively started the city of Inverness when they made their settlement on top of Craig Phadrig, were a group of Celtic tribes who lived in the northern and eastern regions of what was later to become Scotland. Not a great deal is known about them, but they were living in this area before the Romans arrived in Britain in AD 43. They spoke their own language, Pictish, which has not survived, and were superb craftsmen, producing intricate carvings on stone and clay – from graceful animal art to the mysterious symbol stones that are found throughout the region. Some fine examples of these can be seen in the Groam House Museum on the Black Isle (see page 87). You can also learn more about the Picts in the Inverness Museum and Art Gallery (see page 48). The Pictish culture died out in the 10th century when they merged with the more dominant Gaels who had come over from Ireland.

◐ *The Caledonian Canal near Fort Augustus*

OUT OF TOWN
trips

Around Loch Ness

The Caledonian Canal connects the city to one of Scotland's largest and best-known lochs, Loch Ness. Here visitors can take a cruise on the loch to the impressive ruins of Urquhart Castle; watch the boats navigating the flight of locks at Fort Augustus; or visit Drumnadrochit to discover more about the mysterious 'Nessie' – as the Loch Ness Monster is familiarly known.

GETTING THERE

It's about a 55-minute drive down the busy, winding A82 along the west side to Fort Augustus, 55 km (34 miles) away. For a more leisurely drive, you can take the much slower, narrow B852, which hugs the shore on the east side of the loch (follow the B862 from the city towards Dores). You can also visit Drumnadrochit and Fort Augustus by public bus, and there are numerous guided tours from Inverness, including Jacobite Cruises (see pages 67–8), which sail down the Caledonian Canal into Loch Ness.

SIGHTS & ATTRACTIONS

Caledonian Canal

The Caledonian Canal is a 97-km (60-mile) waterway that runs from Fort William on the west coast to the Moray Firth at Inverness, providing an inland passage from sea to sea. It connects the freshwater lochs of the **Great Glen**, a geological

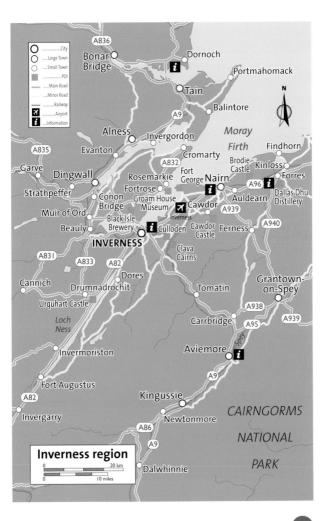

fault that divides the Northwest Highlands from the Grampian Mountains. It was built to avoid the dangers of shipwreck on the long, stormy sea route around the north of Scotland.

Lochs Ness, Oich and Lochy make up 61 km (38 miles) of the canal, but 35 km (22 miles) had to be dug by hand. Designed

🔺 *Clan Urquhart's seat on Loch Ness*

by Thomas Telford, the route required 29 locks. Work began in 1803 and took 20 years to complete. Passenger paddle steamers soon began operating on the canal, bringing tourism to the Highlands. Queen Victoria travelled the canal on the paddle steamer *Gondolier* in 1873.

Drumnadrochit

The tourist hub of Loch Ness is bustling with souvenir shops, tour coaches and a variety of accommodation. It also has two Loch Ness Monster visitor attractions. The **Original Loch Ness Monster Visitor Centre** (ⓐ Loch Ness Lodge Hotel ⓣ 01456 450342 ⓦ www.lochness-centre.com ⓛ 09.00–21.00 daily (May–Sept); 09.00–18.00 daily (Oct–Apr) ⓘ Admission charge) claims to believe in the monster and backs it up with an exhibition on the various sightings and scientific expeditions to find Nessie. The **Loch Ness Exhibition Centre** (ⓐ Drumnadrochit Hotel ⓣ 01456 450573 ⓦ www.lochness.com ⓛ 09.30–17.00 (Feb–May); 09.00–18.00 (Jun & Sept); 09.00–18.30 (Jul & Aug); 09.30–17.00 Oct; 10.00–16.00 (Nov–Jan) ⓘ Admission charge) presents a multimedia experience that aims to debunk the myth. **Loch Ness Cruises** will take you out on the Nessie Hunter, equipped with sonar, underwater camera and other equipment, to search for the monster yourself. ⓐ Original Loch Ness Monster Visitor Centre ⓣ 01456 450395 ⓦ www.lochness-cruises.com ⓛ Easter–December daily (times vary)

Fort Augustus

At the southern tip of Loch Ness, Fort Augustus is the best place to see the Caledonian Canal in action. Here, boats make their

way through an impressive flight of five locks. The little town is a peaceful place to stay and a good base. Find out about the network of local walking and cycle routes at the **Caledonian Canal Visitor Centre** (01463 725500 www.scottishcanals.co.uk 10.00–13.30, 14.00–17.30 daily (Mar–Oct)) beside the locks, where there is a free exhibition about the building of the canal.

A delightful spot for all ages is the **Highland & Rare Breeds Croft** (Rowan Lea, Auchterawe Road, off the A82 in the town centre 01320 366433 daily (Mar–Oct) Admission charge), where you can see a variety of rabbits, poultry, sheep, cattle and deer in a peaceful setting along the riverside. There's also a children's farm. **Cruise Loch Ness**, beside the swing bridge, offers day and evening scenic cruises, sightseeing excursions and a Nessie hunting trip. 01320 366277 www.cruiselochness.com Mar–Jan, boats and times vary.

For more information on the area, visit the helpful **Tourist Information Centre.** A82 in the town centre 0845 622 55121 09.00–17.00 Mon–Sat, 10.00–16.00 Sun (end May–Oct).

Loch Ness

Loch Ness is 227 m (745 ft) at its deepest point. Its great depth makes it the largest Scottish loch by volume. Loch Ness's murky appearance is caused by the high content of peat and mud in the water, furthering its reputation as Nessie's lair. See www.visitlochness.com for advice on what to do on your visit; the site has information on walks, boat trips, golfing, accommodation, eating out and much more.

Urquhart Castle

Sprawled across a rocky promontory above Loch Ness, these impressive ruins were once among Scotland's largest and most important strongholds. The castle dates from the 13th century and underwent many changes until it was blown up by departing government forces, in 1692, to prevent it falling into Jacobite hands. The Visitor Centre contains interesting displays on life at the castle and artefacts found there. The ten-minute film with a surprise ending is the best way to start your visit. ⓐ A82 near Drumnadrochit ⓣ 01456 450551 ⓦ www.historic-scotland.gov.uk ⓒ 09.30–18.00 daily (Apr–Sept); 09.30–17.00 (Oct); 09.30–16.30 (Nov–Mar) ⓘ Admission charge

⏶ *The Loch Ness Exhibition Centre at Drumnadrochit*

RETAIL THERAPY

The Clansman Centre Celtic and Highland crafts and Scottish armoury are sold in this small shop, set in an old monastery chapel beside the canal. ⓐ Fort Augustus ❶ 01320 366444 ⓦ www.scottish-swords.com 🕐 10.00–18.00 daily (Apr–Oct)

Iceberg Glass Beautifully coloured pieces of jewellery, vases and candle holders are produced in this glass-blowing studio a few steps from the canal. ⓐ Main Road, Fort Augustus ❶ 01456 450601 ⓦ www.icebergglass.com 🕐 10.00–20.00 daily (summer); 10.00–18.00 Tues–Sun (spring, autumn); phone first in winter

The Whisky Shop This amazing place sells over a thousand different Scottish whiskies, along with Scottish ales, beers, sweets and foodstuffs. ⓐ Loch Ness Exhibition Centre, Drumnadrochit ❶ 01456 450321 ⓦ www.lochness.com 🕐 10.00–18.00 daily (summer); 10.00–16.00 daily (winter)

TAKING A BREAK

The Brasserie Restaurant ££ In contrast to the traditional feel of the hotel of which it's a part, the Brasserie is a very modern, light and airy eating place that has earned several awards for its cooking. The wine list is reasonably priced, too. ⓐ The Lovat, Fort Augustus ❶ 01456 459250 ⓦ www.thelovat.com 🕐 18.00–21.00 daily (check with restaurant off-season as times may vary) Ⓝ Bus: to Fort Augustus

East of Inverness

A host of attractions lie a short drive east of Inverness. From the historic battlefield at Culloden to the beaches at Nairn to the history of whisky making in Forres, they make for quick and easy day trips from the city.

GETTING THERE

Forres is 43 km (27 miles) from Inverness, about a 45-minute drive on the A96. By car is quickest and easiest, but Nairn and Forres are on the main train line from Inverness to Aberdeen, and most sights can be reached by public bus. For information on the many guided tours, check with the Tourist Office.

SIGHTS & ATTRACTIONS

Cawdor Castle

The Cawdor family still inhabit this romantic medieval castle, but you can cross the drawbridge and tour its historic rooms, winding passageways and the atmospheric Thorn Tree room. Despite its connection with Shakespeare's *Macbeth*, the castle actually dates from the late 14th century, long after Macbeth was crowned High King of Scots in 1040. Afterwards, stroll in the beautiful gardens or follow the nature trails through the ancient trees in Cawdor Big Wood.
ⓐ On the B9090 off the A96 ⓣ 01667 404401
ⓦ www.cawdorcastle.com ⓛ 10.00–17.30 daily (May–first Sun in Oct) ⓝ Bus: 1, X1, 252 ⓘ Admission charge

Clava Cairns

Three ancient burial cairns, surrounded by stone circles, are set in a peaceful shaded grove. You can walk into one of the passage graves. Dating from 2000 BC, they were once part of a much larger Bronze Age burial site. ⓐ Signposted from the B9091, 1.6 km (1 mile) east of Culloden ⓦ www.historic-scotland.gov.uk ⓛ Open access ⓝ Bus: 1 from city centre to Culloden, then a long walk

Culloden

Culloden Moor was the last stand of Bonnie Prince Charlie's Jacobite forces in 1746, and the bloody slaughter on this battlefield was a turning point in Scottish history. The excellent visitor centre tells the story of events before and after the battle, and touch-screens enable you to hear eyewitness accounts from both government and Jacobite supporters. Afterwards, walk the battlefield itself with an audio guide that explains what happened where.
ⓐ B9006, 8 km (5 miles) east of Inverness ⓣ 0844 493 2159 ⓦ www.nts.org.uk ⓛ 09.00–18.00 daily (Apr–Oct); 10.00–16.00 daily (24 Jan–Mar & Nov–23 Dec) ⓝ Bus: 1 from city centre ⓘ Admission charge

Forres

Attractive stone buildings and floral displays line the main streets of this busy market town. Drive to the eastern edge to see **Sueno's Stone**, an impressive 9th-century Pictish stone standing 6 m (20 ft) high and engraved with a battle scene. In the town centre, climb to the top of the **Nelson Tower** for great

views over the Moray Firth. ⓐ Grant Park ⓒ 14.00–16.00 Tues–
Sun (May–Sept)

Brodie Castle is a 16th-century tower house, full of art
and antiques. You can explore the grounds to see the wildlife
hides and enjoy a fine collection of daffodils in spring. ⓐ Off A96
ⓣ 0844 493 2156 ⓦ www.nts.org.uk ⓒ 10.30–16.30 daily (Apr);
10.30–16.30 Sun–Wed (May, Jun, Sept & Oct); 10.30–17.00 daily
(Jul & Aug) ⓘ Admission charge

Though it's no longer a working distillery, a tour of **Dallas
Dhu Distillery** shows you the process of making malt whisky
step by step. Afterwards, enjoy a 'wee dram' (a small measure) in
the tasting room. ⓐ Mannachie Road, Forres ⓣ 01309 676548
ⓦ www.dallasdhu.com ⓔ info@dallasdhu.com ⓒ 09.30–17.30
daily (Apr–Sept); 09.30–16.30 daily (Oct); 09.30–16.30 Sat–Wed
(Nov–Mar) ⓝ Train or bus to Forres then a 15-minute walk
ⓘ Admission charge

🔺 *Brodie Castle was built in 1567 and expanded by William Burn in 1824*

Fort George

This huge, impressive fortress was built in 1748–69 following the Jacobite defeat at Culloden, and still serves as an army barracks. Its formidable bastions and original garrison buildings are handsomely preserved and house a regimental museum and the Seafield Collection of arms. ❸ 18 km (11 miles) northeast of Inverness off the A96 ❶ 01667 460232 Ⓦ www.historic-scotland.gov.uk ❺ 09.30–17.30 daily (Apr–Sept); 09.30–16.30 daily (Oct–Mar) ❶ Admission charge

Nairn

The old fishing port and market town of Nairn is now a popular seaside resort 26 km (16 miles) from Inverness. Its wide, white-sand beach is backed by dunes and a long Victorian promenade, complete with a quaint bandstand. Bottlenose dolphins can often be spotted offshore. Follow the narrow streets of Fishertown, Nairn's ancient fishing quarter, running down to the harbour, and learn more about its history at the **Nairn Museum**, which has a broad collection of photographs, memorabilia and displays. ❸ Viewfield Drive ❶ 01667 456791 Ⓦ www.nairnmuseum.co.uk ❺ 10.00–16.30 Mon–Fri, 10.00–13.00 Sat (Apr–Oct); visits by arrangement only in winter ❶ Admission charge

Nairn has two championship golf courses. The **Nairn Golf Club** (see page 22) dates back to 1887 and is considered to be one of the finest traditional links courses. Nairn hosts several big summer events, including the Book and Arts Festival in June, the International Jazz Festival in August, and one of the region's largest Highland Games.

RETAIL THERAPY

Brodie Country Fare Menswear, women's fashions, accessories, home furnishings, toys and a food hall are among the range of quality goods at this family-run store near Brodie Castle. 🅰 Brodie, near Forres ☎ 01309 641555 🌐 www.brodiecountryfare.com 🕒 09.30–17.30 daily (summer); 09.30–17.00 (winter)

Logie Steading The converted farm buildings house a second-hand bookshop, art gallery, furniture, antiques, designer bags, accessories, and a farm and garden shop. An adventure playground keeps kids amused. 🅰 A940/B9007 south of Forres 🌐 www.logie.co.uk 🕒 10.30–17.00 daily (Mar–Christmas)

TAKING A BREAK

Blue Angel Café £ In the heart of the Findhorn Foundation, the café serves organic and vegetarian fare, and has a pleasant outdoor deck. ☎ 01309 691900 🌐 www.blueangelcafe.co.uk 🕒 10.00–17.00 daily 🚌 Bus: 10A, 11 to Forres

Sea View Restaurant ££ With lovely views across the greens and sand dunes of Nairn to the Moray Firth beyond, this is a bright and light-filled restaurant, offering simple dishes like fish and chips, Scottish salmon, and pepper steak. 🅰 Braeval Hotel, Crescent Road, Nairn ☎ 01667 452341 🌐 www.braevalhotel.co.uk 📧 info@braevalhotel.co.uk 🕒 18.00–21.00 daily 🚌 Bus: 10a, 11 to Nairn

The Black Isle & Dornoch

North of Inverness, the Black Isle beckons across the Moray Firth. This rural peninsula, with its rolling hills and pretty villages, makes for lovely driving country and has several good spots for dolphin watching. Further north, Dornoch, with its renowned golf course and beautiful beaches, makes a good base for scenic drives in the Highlands.

GETTING THERE

Cromarty, at the northeast tip of the Black Isle, is about 37 km (23 miles) from Inverness, a 40-minute drive without stops. Dornoch is 77 km (48 miles) from Inverness, about an hour's drive on the A9. There is a public bus service to Rosemarkie and Cromarty on the Black Isle, and buses to Dornoch. Check with the Tourist Information Office for details of the various sightseeing excursions to the Black Isle.

SIGHTS & ATTRACTIONS

Beauly

Before the bridge across the Moray Firth was built, the main route to the Black Isle went through this attractive town. In the town centre, visit the atmospheric ruins of **Beauly Priory**. ⓐ Off High Street ⓣ 01663 783444 ⓦ www.historic-scotland.gov.uk ⓛ 10.00–16.00 daily

North of town, the **Glen Ord Distillery** gives tours year-round. ⓐ A862, Muir of Ord ⓣ 01463 872004 ⓦ www.discovering-

distilleries.com/glenord ⏱ 10.00–17.00 Mon–Fri, 11.00–17.00 Sat
(Apr–Sept); Sun 12.00–16.00 (Jul–Sept); 11.00–16.00 Mon–Fri
(Oct–Mar) ❶ Admission charge

The **Beauly Centre** has exhibits on regional history and
culture as well as tourist information. Ask too about the
beautiful scenic drives south through Strathglass and Glen
Affric. ⓐ High Street

Black Isle Brewery

Located on a family farm that has been cultivating barley
since 1790, Black Isle Brewery produces a range of six organic
beers and special seasonal beers. There are free tours and
tastings all year. ⓐ Signposted off A9, near Munlochy ❶ 01463
811871 ⓦ www.blackislebrewery.com ⏱ 10.00–18.00 Mon–Sat
(year-round); 11.30–17.00 Sun (Apr–Sept)

Cromarty

With its fine natural harbour, Cromarty was a prosperous
18th-century fishing and trading port. One of Scotland's first
factories, the hemp works, was built here in 1774. The town
contains many handsome merchants' houses and historic
buildings. The **Hugh Miller Museum and Birthplace Cottage**
(ⓐ Church Street ❶ 0844 493 2158 ⓦ www.hughmiller.org
⏱ 13.00–17.00 Sun–Wed (May–Sept); 13.00–17.00 Sun & Tues
(Oct) ❶ Admission charge) contains memorabilia of the
geologist and writer who was born here in 1802. The **Cromarty
Courthouse** is now a museum, where you can watch
animatronic figures re-enact a trial in the old courtroom.
ⓐ Church Street ❶ 01381 600418

ⓦ www.cromarty-courthouse.org.uk ⓛ 11.00–16.00 Sun–Thur
(Easter–Oct) ⓘ Admission charge

Dolphin watching

Just across the bridge in North Kessock, beside the **Tourist
Information Centre** (ⓐ Picnic site, North Kessock ⓣ 0845 225 5121
ⓛ 10.00–17.00 Mon–Sat, Sun 10.00–16.00 (Mar–early Oct)), the
Dolphin & Seal Visitor Centre (ⓣ 01463 731866 ⓛ 09.30–16.30
daily (Jun–Sept)) is one of the best places to spot wildlife.
Bottlenose dolphins are regularly seen in the channel below,
particularly in the summer when they hunt for migrating

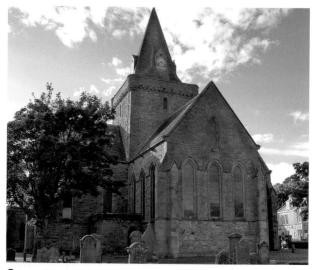

🔺 *Dornoch Cathedral dates from the 16th and 19th centuries*

salmon. At about 4 m (13 ft) long, these are the largest bottlenose dolphins in the world and are part of the resident population in the Moray Firth. Common dolphins, harbour seals, grey heron and other wildlife are also occasionally seen.

Another good place for dolphin spotting is Chanonry Point (follow signs from the A832 at Fortrose). **Dolphin Trips Avoch** offer wildlife cruises in these waters from the harbour at nearby Avoch. ⓐ Harbourside, Avoch ⓣ 01381 622383 ⓦ www.dolphintripsavoch.co.uk ⓛ Hourly sailings Easter–Oct (depending on demand, tide and weather) ⓘ Admission charge

Dornoch

Bordered by two championship golf courses overlooking the Dornoch Firth, Dornoch is often called the St Andrews of the North. One of these, the **Royal Dornoch**, is considered to be one of the finest links courses in the world. ⓐ Golf Road ⓣ 01862 810219 ⓦ www.royaldornoch.com

Dornoch also has sweeping sandy beaches, which make it a popular holiday resort. The town's attractive sandstone buildings are centred around the cathedral, built in the 13th century. Opposite is the 15th-century Dornoch Castle, now a hotel.

CULTURE

Groam House Museum

This small museum in an 18th-century house is well worth a visit for its collection of carved Pictish stones. The centrepiece is the Rosemarkie Stone, a cross-slab standing nearly 3 m (10 ft) tall. Other exhibits give an insight into the history and culture

of the Picts. ⓐ High Street, Rosemarkie ⓣ 01381 620961
ⓦ www.groamhouse.org.uk ⓛ 10.00–17.00 Mon–Sat, 14.00–16.30
Sun (May–Oct); 14.00–16.00 Sat & Sun (Nov–mid-Dec, Mar & Apr);
14.00–16.30 daily (Easter week) ⓝ Bus: 26, 26A from Inverness

RETAIL THERAPY

Jail Dornoch Opposite the cathedral, Dornoch's 19th-century
jail now houses an attractive shop selling art, ceramics,
clothing, jewellery and gifts. ⓐ Castle Street ⓣ 01862 810500
ⓦ www.jail-dornoch.com ⓛ 09.00–18.00 Mon–Sat, 10.00–17.00
Sun (summer); 09.30–17.00 Mon–Sat, 11.00–17.00 Sun (winter)

Storehouse of Foulis Fresh Black Isle produce and delectable
deli items are sold at this farm shop and restaurant, next to
a restored 18th-century storehouse on the Cromarty Firth.
ⓐ A9, Evanton ⓣ 01349 830038 ⓦ www.storehouseoffoulis.co.uk
ⓛ 09.00–18.00 Mon–Sat, 10.00–17.00 Sun

TAKING A BREAK

Dornoch Castle £££ Dine in the cosy bar with its 15th-century
stone walls or in the bright and spacious conservatory-style
Garden Restaurant. Enjoy the creatively prepared traditional
dishes such as Highland venison, Loch Duart salmon or the local
Dornoch Firth mussels. ⓐ Castle Street, Dornoch ⓣ 01862 810216
ⓦ www.dornochcastlehotel.com ⓝ Bus: X99 to Dornoch

◗ *Part of the Bronze Age cemetery at Clava Cairns*

PRACTICAL
information

Directory

GETTING THERE
By air

Inverness Airport is served by several airlines, with flights from London and several regional British airports, the main ones being easyJet (ⓦ www.easyjet.com) and Flybe (ⓦ www.flybe.com).

Inverness Airport ⓐ Dalcross, Inverness ⓣ 01667 464000 ⓕ 01667 462041 ⓦ www.hial.co.uk/inverness-airport ⓛ 05.30–22.00 daily ⓝ JET bus service to city centre

Many people are aware that air travel emits CO_2, which contributes to climate change. You may be interested in the possibility of lessening the environmental impact of your flight through the charity **Climate Care** (ⓦ www.jpmorganclimatecare.com), which offsets your CO_2 by funding environmental projects around the world.

By bus

There are daily buses to Inverness from Edinburgh and Glasgow with **Scottish CityLink** (ⓣ 08705 505050 ⓦ www.citylink.co.uk) and **Megabus** (ⓣ 0900 160 0900 ⓦ www.megabus.com), and daily services to Glasgow with National Express (ⓣ 08717 818178 ⓦ www.nationalexpress.com).

By car

There are no motorways in this part of Scotland, the closest being the M90 which ends at Perth, a 176-km (110-mile) drive south of Inverness. The main road to Inverness is the A9, which is mostly a fast road but can be slower when summer brings more visitors to the region. From Edinburgh to Inverness takes just over three hours, on the M90 as far as Perth and then on the A9. Glasgow takes about half an hour longer; leave the city on the M80 and later, take the M9 to the A9 just beyond Stirling.

By rail

There are daily direct trains from Edinburgh and Glasgow to Inverness, taking 3–4 hours. The Caledonian Sleeper service leaves London Euston for Inverness every night except Saturday, and takes 12.5 hours. All bookings with ScotRail (ℹ 0845 755 0033 ⓦ www.scotrail.co.uk).

GETTING AROUND

Car hire

Budget ⓐ Burns Cottage, Railway Terrace, Inverness
ⓣ 01463 713333 ⓦ www.budget.co.uk
Focus Vehicle Rental ⓐ Inverness Airport, Unit 14A, Dalcross Industrial Estate, Inverness ⓣ 01667 461212 ⓕ 01667 461212
ⓦ www.focusvehiclerental.co.uk
Thrifty ⓐ 33 Harbour Road, Inverness ⓣ 01463 224466
ⓦ www.thrifty.co.uk ⓔ thrifty.inverness@thrifty.co.uk
Top Car Car Hire ⓐ 1 Harbour Road, Inverness ⓣ 01463 713880
ⓦ www.topcarinverness.com ⓔ top.car@btconnect.com

Taxis

City Taxis ⓐ Unit 6, 7A Canal Road, Inverness ⓣ 01463 222555
ⓦ www.citytaxisinverness.co.uk ⓔ enquiries@citytaxisinverness.co.uk

Highland Taxis ⓐ Farraline Park, Inverness ⓣ 01463 222222
ⓦ www.highlandtaxis.co.uk ⓔ info@highlandtaxis.co.uk

HEALTH, SAFETY & CRIME

Crime is no better or worse in Inverness than in any other British
city of its size. Take the usual safety precautions you would
anywhere: don't leave valuables in cars, don't leave bags
unattended and keep an eye on your handbag or wallet in
busy public places.

There are no particular health issues to worry about.
The worst hazard is the summer arrival of the Highland
midges. Take insect repellent and check this website before
going: ⓦ http://2010.midgeforecast.co.uk

Ambulance, Fire, Police ⓣ 999
Academy Dental Practice ⓐ 19 Union Street, Inverness
ⓣ 01463 232423, 01463 233187
Raigmore Hospital ⓐ Old Perth Road, Inverness ⓣ 01463 704000
ⓝ Bus: 3, 3A, 3B, 4, 4A
Riverside Medical Practice ⓐ Ballifeary Lane, Ness Walk,
Inverness ⓣ 01463 715999

For other options, check the website of the Highlands
region of the National Health Service:
ⓦ www.nhshighland.scot.nhs.uk

OPENING HOURS

Most shops open from 09.00 to 17.00 or 18.00. Larger retail
centres are also open on Sundays, from 11.00–17.00, and some
shops in the centre will open on Sundays in summer. Banks are

open between 09.00 or 09.15 and 16.45 or 17.00 Monday to Friday; many open slightly later on a Wednesday morning.

CHILDREN

Inverness is a very child-friendly place. Attractions for children include **Bogbain Adventure Heritage Park** (ⓐ Bogbain Farm, Inches, Inverness ❶ 01463 772800 ⓦ www.bogbainfarm.com ⓔ info@bogbainfarm.com ❶ 10.00–18.30 daily ◉ Bus: 4); **Inverness Museum and Art Gallery** (see page 48); **Ness Islands Railway** (ⓐ Whin Park ❶ 01463 235533 ⓦ www.nessislandsrailway.co.uk ❶ 11.00–16.30 daily during local school holidays, 11.00–16.30 Sat & Sun (Easter–Oct) ❶ All openings are subject to the weather; Admission charge).

TRAVELLERS WITH DISABILITIES

Newer hotels and attractions such as the Inverness Museum have wheelchair access and facilities for travellers with disabilities. There is a disabled toilet inside the Victorian Market.

Visitors to Inverness who have the local equivalent of a Blue Badge, entitling them to disabled parking access, can apply for a permit for equivalent parking in Inverness on payment of a fee of £20. Further details ⓦ www.highland.gov.uk

FURTHER INFORMATION

Inverness Tourist Information Centre ⓐ Castle Wynd, Inverness ❶ 01463 234353 ⓦ www.visithighlands.com ❶ 09.00–18.00 Mon–Sat, 09.30–16.00 Sun (26 May–end Jun & 1–14 Sept); 09.00–18.00 Mon–Sat, 09.00–17.00 Sun (Jul & Aug); 09.00–17.00 Mon–Sat, 10.00–16.00 Sun (15 Sept–end Dec & Apr–25 May)

ACKNOWLEDGEMENTS

The photographs in this book were taken by Cezare White for Thomas Cook Publishing, to whom the copyright belongs, except for the following: flickr.com page 16 (brianholsclaw); iStockphoto pages 9 (Carney05), 12 (Matphoto), 13 (mammamaart), 21, 74 (TT), 41 (Richard Cliff), 45 (Gannet77); Shutterstock pages 5 (aeropus), 7 (Tikky), 66 (Uriel M Ulam), 71 (Angelina Dimitrova), 86 (Stephen Beaumont); Wikimedia Commons pages 31 (Stefan.gotte), 66 (Gregory J Kingsley), 89 (Unukorno).

Project editor: Rosalind Munro
Copy editor: Penny Isaac
Proofreaders: Michele Greenbank & Ceinwen Sinclair
Layout: Julie Crane
Indexer: Penelope Kent

AUTHOR BIOGRAPHY

Mike Gerrard and Donna Dailey are award-winning travel writers who have written more than 50 travel guides and inspirational travel books, including Thomas Cook's *driving guides Scotland*. Their articles and photographs covering European, US and worldwide destinations appear in a variety of magazines, newspapers and websites, including their own website: www.Pacific-Coast-Highway-Travel.com

Send your thoughts to
books@thomascook.com

- Found a great bar, club, shop or must-see sight that we don't feature?

- Like to tip us off about any information that needs a little updating?

- Want to tell us what you love about this handy little guidebook and more importantly how we can make it even handier?

Then here's your chance to tell all! Send us ideas, discoveries and recommendations today and then look out for your valuable input in the next edition of this title.

Email the above address (stating the title) or write to:
pocket guides Series Editor, Thomas Cook Publishing, PO Box 227, Coningsby Road, Peterborough PE3 8SB, UK.